Structures Up Close

Look Closely!

by Wiley Blevins

LOOK! BOOKS™

Red Chair Press Egremont, Massachusetts

Look! Books are produced and published by Red Chair Press:

Red Chair Press LLC PO Box 333 South Egremont, MA 01258-0333

www.redchairpress.com

FREE Educator Guides at www.redchairpress.com/free-resources

Publisher's Cataloging-In-Publication Data
Names: Blevins, Wiley.
Title: Structures up close / by Wiley Blevins.

Description: Egremont, Massachusetts : Red Chair Press, [2019] | Series: Look! books. Look closely | Interest age level: 004-007. | Includes Now You Know fact-boxes, a glossary, and resources for additional reading. | Includes index. | Summary: "In Structures Up Close, young readers view a portion of a well-known structure or building. Readers learn what makes the structure unique and interesting."--Provided by publisher.

Identifiers: ISBN 9781634406673 (library hardcover) | ISBN 9781634406710 (paperback) | ISBN 9781634406758 (ebook)

Subjects: LCSH: Buildings--Juvenile literature. | CYAC: Buildings.

Classification: LCC TH149 .B54 2019 (print) | LCC TH149 (ebook) | DDC 690 [E]--dc23

LCCN: 2018955657

Photo credits: cover, pp. 1, 6, 8, 10, 10–11, 14, 16, 18, 20, 21, 22 Shutterstock; pp. 4, 6–7, 12, 15, 24 iStock; p. 19 © Design Pics Inc/Alamy.

Printed in United States of America

0519 1P CGF19

Table of Contents

The photo shows part of a building or structure. What is it? Look for clues in the riddle!

Standing Tall!

This is big and green. It watches over a **harbor**. It welcomes visitors. What is it?

It's the Statue of Liberty. You can see it in New York City. It was a gift from France. The nose is over 4 feet long!

GOOD to KNOW

The Statue of Liberty is also called "Lady Liberty".

JULY
IV

8

More Than a Shape

It's shaped like a triangle. It's very big and made of stone. It rises up from the **desert**. You can even ride a camel to see it. What is it?

It is the Great Pyramid of Giza. It's in Egypt. Long ago, pharaohs(*fer-ohs*) were buried inside. They were kings of **ancient** Egypt.

GOOD to KNOW

Each stone block weighs more than a car.

The pyramids in Giza were built nearly 5,000 years ago!

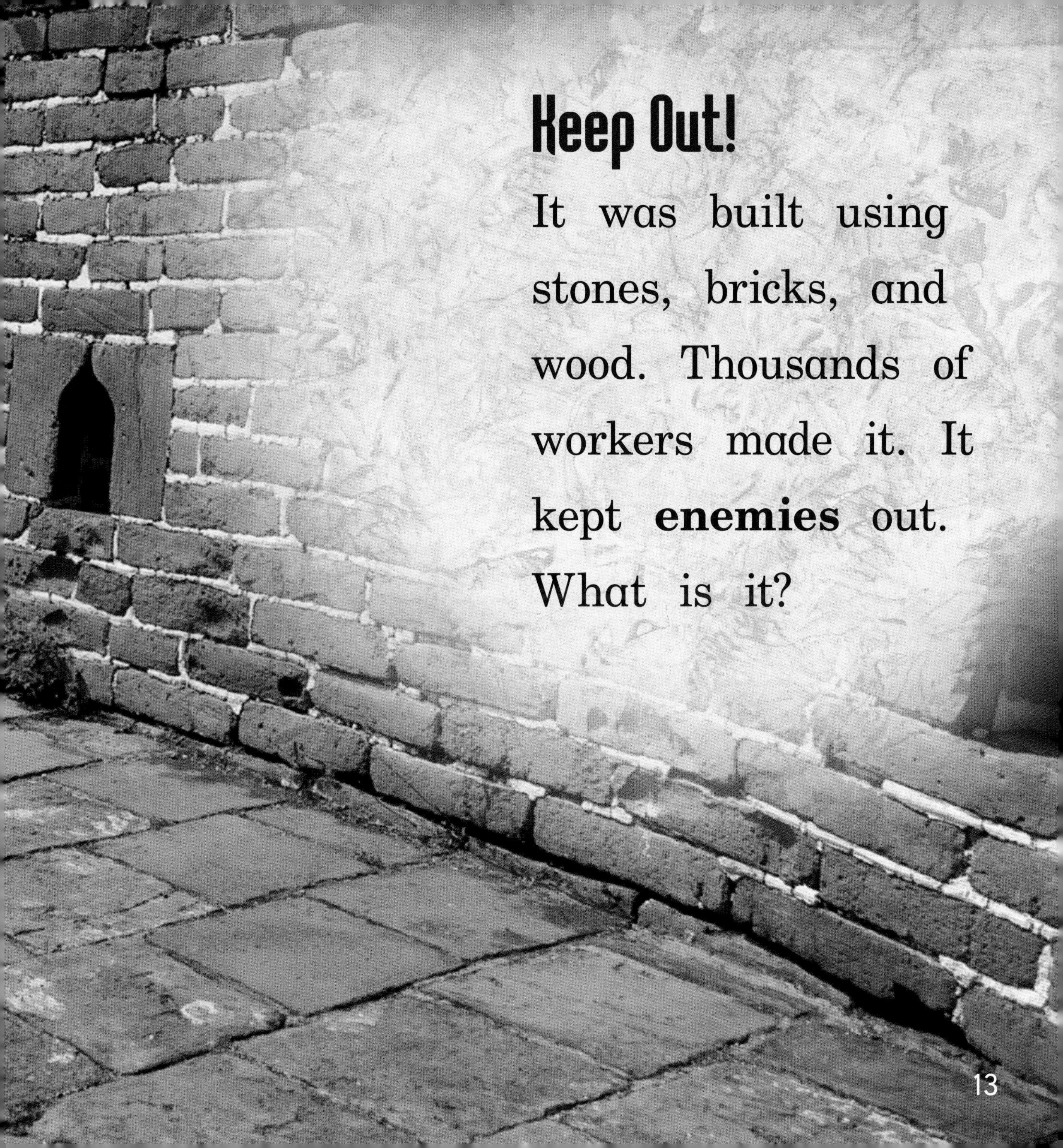

Keep Out!

It was built using stones, bricks, and wood. Thousands of workers made it. It kept **enemies** out. What is it?

It's the Great Wall of China. It stretches over 5,000 miles. Lookout towers helped soldiers see when raiders were ready to attack.

GOOD to KNOW

This wall was named one of the New Seven Wonders of the World.

The Great Wall of China is longer than the distance from New York to California.

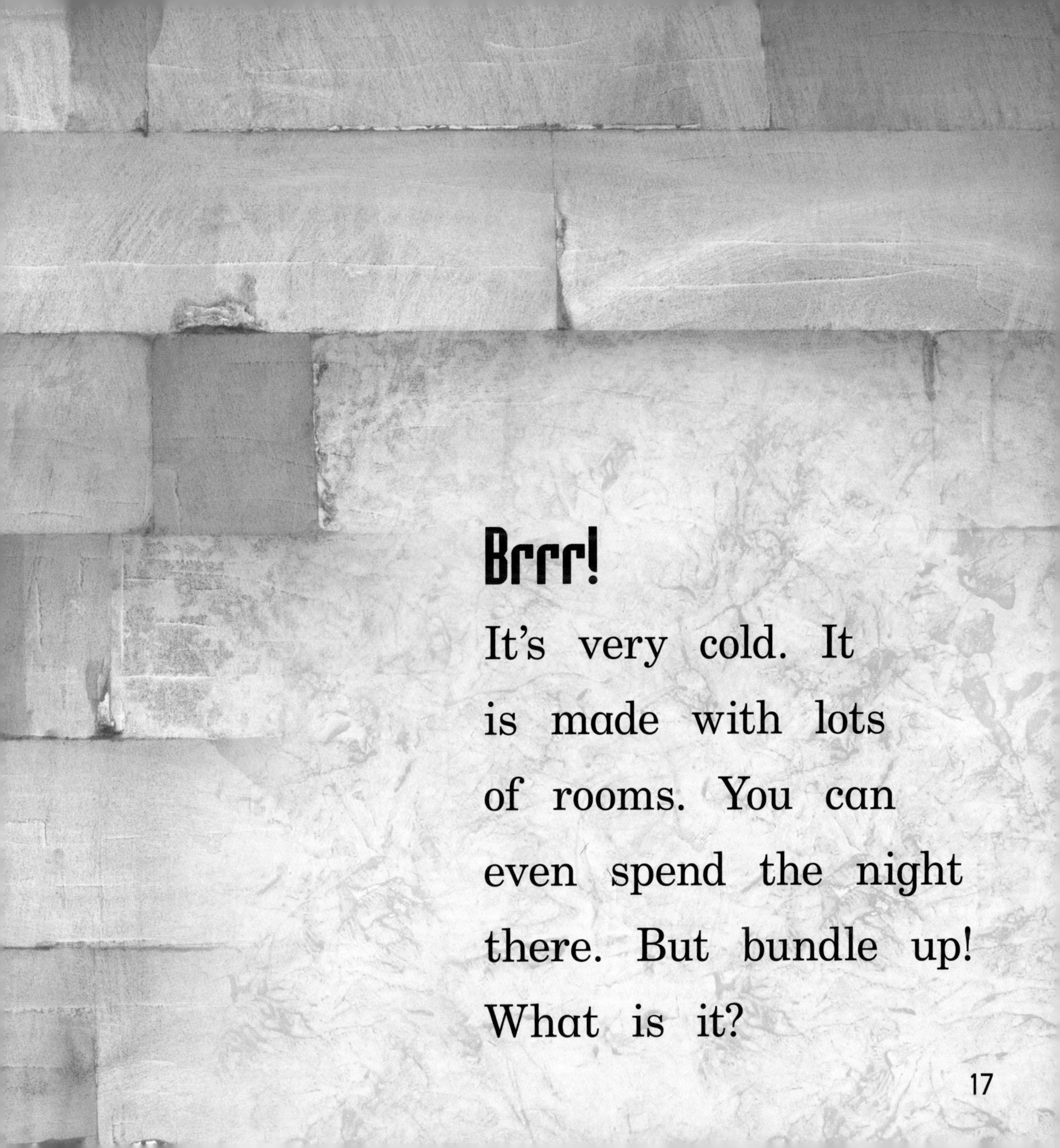

Brrr!

It's very cold. It is made with lots of rooms. You can even spend the night there. But bundle up! What is it?

It's the Ice **Hotel** in Canada. It's made of snow and ice. You can rent a room here from January to March. It even has an ice slide inside to get around. Make sure you visit before it melts in Spring!

Inside the Ice Hotel with an ice bed!

Test Yourself!

What are these buildings or structures? Where are they? There are no clues. But look closely! Each is famous all over the world.

2

3

1
The White House

2
Neuschwanstein
Castle

3
Machu Picchu

Words to Keep

ancient: very old

desert: a place with little water and plants, often covered by sand

enemies: people who are not friends and want to harm you

harbor: a place on the coast where ships can park and stay safe

hotel: a place where you can rent a room when you're traveling

Learn More at the Library

Books (Check out these books to learn more.)

Hayden, Kate. *Amazing Buildings.* DK Readers, 2003.

Stanborough, Rebecca J. *Great Wall of China.* Capstone Press, 2016.

Marsh, Laura. *Pyramids.* National Geographic Readers, 2017

Web sites (Ask an adult to show you these web sites.)

Egypt: Pyramids (National Geographic Kids)

https://www.youtube.com/watch?v=FIt8ZXFev2Y

China: Great Wall (National Geographic Kids)

https://www.youtube.com/watch?v=IuDvAJhnoxM

Index

About the Author

Wiley Blevins has written many books for kids. He lives in New York City where the Statue of Liberty can be found.